Living Inside the Rainbow
Workbook & Study Journal Companion

A Faith-based Approach

Dr. Brook Parker Bello
Living Inside the Rainbow
Workbook & Study Journal
Companion

A Faith-based Approach
Based on the educational Living Inside the
Rainbow Winning the Battlefield of the Mind after
Human Trafficking & Mental Bondage

All scripture quotations, unless otherwise indicated are taken from the King James Version (KJV) of the Holy Bible. Scriptures marked (AMP) are taken from the Amplified Bible Copyright © 1954, 1958, 1962, 1964, 1965, 1987 by The Lockman Foundation. Used by permission.

For Information on Dr. Bello's soul health getaways and for ministry, teaching and speaking engagements please visit brookbello.com or therapyoffthegrid.com

To join the fight to stop human trafficking and end demand please visit us at
www.moretoolife.org
Follow us on Twitter: @BrookBello
Follow Brook on Facebook.com/brook.bello
Email Us for Speaking Engagements: exec_a@moretoolife.org

Published By:
To Soar Publications Brook Parker Bello
Printed in the United States of America

"Faith is a living, daring confidence in God's grace, so sure and certain that a man could stake his life on it a thousand times."

Martin Luther (1482-1546)

DEDICATION
To my Husband Teddy Bello (Theo)
The man of God and honor who won my heart

CONTENTS

Living Inside the Rainbow
Workbook & Study Journal Companion.
A Faith-based Approach

We are going to assess through the initial understanding of who you are, decide if you or the mentee you are working with needs some form of therapy, mentoring, education on human trafficking, freedom from sexual violence, domestic violence, emotional abuse and other emotionally difficult traumas. In addition, if you are a former gang member and have been involved in hurting others, take note. Sexual abuse, "the life or the death and the game," pimp culture, prostitution, addictions and legal ramifications are important to contemplate as you move forward.

Start to change the mindset of "a *victim*" to understand the root causes and overcome shame and guilt of being a victim. Applying aspects of self-worth, love, and healthy relationships overall.

Emphasis on a holistic therapeutic track, in addition to learning and understanding a survivors' strengths & weaknesses, and educational background in preparation for entry into a transformational new life. So, intensive therapy, psych evaluations, journaling, creative thinking and artistic processes that open victims to express themselves via the word of God and other creative practices such as art, music, painting, and of course, time in worship, prayer and practicing forgiveness and critical thinking. My training videos, the one-on-ones, group mentoring, survivor connections and other practices are important in understanding the survivors' strengths & weaknesses. The curriculum can be ordered later via brookbello.com as the work is implemented through the curriculum which is not part of this book, but you can purchase it separately. But for now, the foundational understanding of who you are and/or those you are assisting based on the faith-based educational journey in Living Inside the Rainbow... will be explored in this new study journal. If you have not read the book this is based on, order Living Inside the Rainbow Winning the Battlefield of the Mind... today. Amazon, iTunes, Kindle, Goodreads and Barnes & Noble. Enjoy the journey.

Intro from the Book:

When you assassinate the soul of an innocent child or a broken woman or man, you are doing far more than making an offense. In fact, you are indulging in one of the most damaging of all crimes and human rights violations known to man. ~ Brook Bello

Peradventure after having read the introduction of my book, *Living Inside the Rainbow: Winning the Battlefield of the Mind After Human Trafficking and Mental Bondage,* you can begin to relate to my story which resonates with many transformational stories around the world, and even your own, regardless of what challenges you have faced. Maybe as a victim or a counselor who has been with several victims, and you are afraid to acknowledge you were once a victim... running from any tendency to remember the incident. Each time you recall the scene, your heart would be broken, filled with regrets and guilt you were not meant to bear.

1. Would you rather acknowledge you were a victim (though it seems like a dream at times and you don't want to wake up to reality), still in need of help? Think of why you might block believing you were a victim and journal how it makes you feel.

_____

_____

_____

_____

_____

_____

_____

_____

Maybe it brings or has brought you suicidal thoughts, mixed feelings, self-hate, and low self-esteem. It signifies you are still hurting—not yet healed. Please think of the times that you have thought that maybe your life was not worth living or if it would be better off if you were gone.

_____

_____

_____

_____

_____

_____

_____

_____

2. Do you often feel a rush of disgust in your heart each time you hear someone talk about the subject of sexual crimes, domestic violence, human trafficking, physical abuse and all its root causes all because it triggers your memory? Please write down when and how.

_____

_____

_____

_____

_____

_____

_____

_____

3. How did you feel when you first saw the title of the main book this workbook is derived from? Did you think of peace and your time of freedom or someone you are supporting? Or did you think of the scriptures it relates to? What does it mean to you? Journal all the scriptures that have the word rainbow in them and reflect on the meaning and how it relates to your life and the life of those you are assisting.

_____

_____

_____

_____

_____

_____

_____

_____

4. Do you still hold bitterness in your heart against those your 'adversaries' who abused you? Or those who have abused others? Then, please consider who you need to forgive and pray for the strength to release them so that you are free.

_____

_____

_____

_____

_____

_____

_____

_____

Forgiveness is one of the most difficult things, and even God directed practices to accomplish, especially after abuse and pain, yet it is our greatest task and the most profound one that actually frees us and takes us deeper into a beautiful relationship with God and a personal relationship with Jesus the Christ and the Holy Spirit.

5. Do you always try to force yourself not to remember the incident or moments when you have been hurt and seem powerless to do anything, thus leading to more frustration? How do you feel in such situations? Name them all and try not to force or push for what you can or cannot remember. Follow the peace of God and discover ways to appreciate who you are today.

_____

_____

_____

_____

_____

_____

_____

_____

To heal, you must come to terms with the facts of the matters that have hurt you and how through love, therapy, pastoral clinical therapy and much prayer and meditation on where you can go and who you are and were born to be and by God's grace and your forgiveness, you can begin a new journey. As you go further through your workbook and study journal, please write, be open and honest with a view to finding keys to your healing.

PART ONE
The Importance of Understanding

Chapter 1

Honesty is Difficult
When We Don't Know the Truth

You're not alone in this. "Everyone heals in their own time and in their own way. The path isn't always a straight line, and you don't need to go it alone." — Zeke Thomas

God is the very definition of science and so wrapped up in all of who He is, as the Creator of heaven and earth, and of course all of this is also science. Yet, scientists focus only on their science, not realizing that they are only starting to uncover what God created!

1. Do you know God was aware of all you went through, or are going through right now if you're still in bondage to a human trafficker or in some other addiction or pain? Please, expand on the thoughts and ideas and begin to critically think about what you are thinking of when you think of God and His all-knowing presence that you might feel didn't rescue you?

_____

_____

_____

_____

_____

_____

_____

_____

2. Would you rather blame God for abandoning you in your struggle with those that hurt you or can you focus on the abusers?

_____

_____

_____

_____

_____

_____

_____

3. In a sincere, simple way, state what you would rather want God to do for you on your emotional and psychological trauma. Hint: Write as though it's a note telling God how bad it hurts and areas you want His healing touch upon you while you're being honest about asking God for the answers of why it happened to you? You must also write down if you have even forgiven yourself and begin to write down why or why not? This will be something that you must do as soon as possible.

_____

_____

_____

_____

_____

_____

_____

4. Is there any life goal that you formed and have held onto while in an abuse that needs to be changed? Is your identity perceived from a life of trauma or are there remnants from the past? Do you seem to have

lost your hold on why you were created in the first place and looking to discover a fresh and entirely new life? Please take your time.

_____

_____

_____

_____

_____

_____

_____

_____

_____

5. Has there been any time you feel the world is cruel after your experience? Perhaps too cruel to remain in?

_____

_____

_____

_____

_____

_____

_____

_____

God can restore lost glory. As a matter of fact, He already has, yet we must be willing to surrender it all over to Him and begin the new life that has already been redeemed for us. 'And I will restore to you the years that the locust hath eaten, the cankerworm, and the caterpillar, and the palmerworm, my great army which I sent among you.' (Joel-2:25)

Reconfigure your mind to take up again your real identity in God. The abuse was a distraction from the Evil one to get you off the track of discovering the true authority and power you truly have. The first person that Evil brainwashed and raped of her identity was Eve (and by extension, Adam). Yet, God didn't abandon them to fate to let them wander through life in nakedness. God clothed them with coats of skin! Read Genesis 3:1-21.

6. In what ways can you describe yourself after having suffered from human trafficking, sex trafficking, exploitation, prostitution, or other forms of abuse, bondage and addictions? Hint: Use specific adjectives and nouns.

_____
_____
_____
_____
_____
_____
_____
_____

7. How can you describe the abuser, violator or trafficker? Think about what you must unlearn. Reading this book set tells that you choose life on some level. How deep can you delve to let go and discover who you really are.

_____
_____
_____
_____
_____
_____
_____
_____

Restorative Justice is a key to healing. The idea that those who hurt you or those who hurt others similar to you can hear how it affected you while you in return can release them and move forward in God's authority and power. If you have an opportunity to meet with abusers, violators or traffickers, how will you relate with them on how you feel? Will you see them, write a letter or simply choose to let it go instead? Think about it and be clear. Note that when abusers know how you feel, even if in a letter, it frees you and sometimes assists them on not hurting others.

_____
_____
_____
_____
_____
_____
_____
_____

9. Whose voice can you hear or see in those words you now describe yourself with? Is there something you'd like to change?

_____
_____
_____
_____
_____
_____
_____
_____

You can continue your healing by accepting and embracing what God has said about you even despite how you may feel about yourself. *Evil, desires for us to stay dead and to keep us from being God's masterpiece. The wicked one works to keep us in that lost state which took place in the Garden.*

Do you believe in God? Do you know what it means to be *born again or born from above*? Is there any way your new birth experience or the thought of it has helped you in your life challenges?

_____

_____

_____

_____

_____

_____

_____

By natural birth (through parents as predefined in creation), you are His *offspring*. By spiritual birth, you're His son/daughter born into the Kingdom of Christ. God is the Higher Power you need to overcome your trauma. Read John 3:1-6; Isaiah 41:10.

11. Do you think it is possible for you to forgive all those that hurt you?

_____

_____

_____

_____

_____

_____

_____

Forgiveness is what you need to overcome the memory of your experience. Read Amos 5:14-15. Continue to journal and lean in to the the Holy Spirit by sitting in a quite place and allowing God to speak to your heart. Listening, is best done in a quiet place and a deeply open posture of longing for and needing God to show up and reveal all you need through Jesus' love and the impressions from the Holy Spirit.

Chapter 2
Love, Hope, and Stamina

God is truly awesome! You know, over time, the Gospels have brought a perpetual healing that, along with cognitive therapy (speaking and being listened to and seeking wisdom), helped me to understand basic boundaries. I was transformed! I realize that it was not an instantaneous healing, but it was a supernatural process.

1. Have you begun to feel the need to share your mind? Thus, your heart with someone you can trust or have you become a person someone else can trust to share their deepest hurt? Be honest. If the answer is no, then why or why not?

_____

_____

_____

_____

_____

_____

_____

_____

2. Has there been any time that you feel like asking your abuser, violator, trafficker/molester the reason for their actions? Even when it is a parent or close family relationship? Remember that many abusers can't answer why but sometimes, it is good to remember if this is a question you have thought of.. Please, write what you'd like to know and ask God if it needs to leave the pages of your journal. God will also give you the answers you need without having to ask those that hurt you.

_____

_____

_____

_____

_____

_____

_____

_____

3. State (if any) why you still feel insecure with low self-esteem and reserved in the presence of others? What are the things that often upset you from building relationships? Do you often transfer aggression on your neighbor, relative, friend? Do you realize that sometimes it's because of the hurtful feelings from your past?

_____

_____

_____

_____

_____

_____

_____

_____

Love is like a fish in the river. The fish drink from the river and also swim in the river. That is the only way for the fish to survive. It needs water within and without. Love also must be within and without.

You must be open to true love if you want to heal from inside out.

"But no matter how much evil I see, I think it's important for everyone to understand that there is much more light than darkness."
— Robert Uttaro

Love God.
Love yourself...
Love others.

Feelings—ugh. I was so concerned about what people thought. The evidence of my concern was that I was afraid to be with others and when I was, I just knew that I was doing something wrong.

You're not your feelings or thoughts or mind; your identity is with God, and you have control over them all. See Romans 8:1-2.

Self-hate, self-condemnation—avoid them like the plague! It's the voice of the enemy and of the abuser, trafficker or violator as a representative of the devil.

4. Mention at least 3-7 people you feel contributed to your hurt.

_____

_____

_____

_____

_____

_____

_____

_____

Did you write your own name there? If not, why not?

_____

_____

_____

_____

_____

_____

_____

_____

Now, by God's grace, release those offenders from your mind by forgiving them and yourself for evil or not knowing or understanding. Pray this:

God, I forgive_____ of the evils they did to me... {from here, pray the prayer that the Holy Spirit leads you into} Note that there are also extraordinary prayer books that have been highly beneficial to me by Bam Crawford, Pastor Sarah Morgan, Dr. Cindy Trimm, and Apostle John Eckhardt. You can also look for my book, "Shame Undone. When Unforgiveness Meets Grace."

6. Write 1 or 2 reasons you think or feel you should heartily do #3 and #4 above.

_____

_____

_____

_____

_____

_____

_____

_____

There would come a time when I would have to forgive the most difficult person in my life, and this is usually the hardest for us all, and that is the self: myself.

7. Have you smelled Roses before or other sweet exotic flowers? How does it 'feel' to your emotions as to the scent thereof?

(Psalm 34:8; ESV) Oh, taste and see that the Lord is good! Blessed is the man who takes refuge in him (Psalm 115:3-8; ESV)! Our God is in the heavens; he does all that he pleases. Their idols are silver and gold, the work of human hands. They have mouths, but do not speak; eyes, but do not see. They have ears, but do not hear; noses, but do not smell. They have hands, but do not feel; feet, but do not walk; and they do not make a sound in their throat.

But... "The hearing ear and the seeing eye, the Lord has made them both" (Proverbs 20:12; ESV).

Practice by describing how all of our senses are at play when we make decisions.

_____

_____

_____

_____

_____

_____

_____

_____

_____

In nature, you can see God's glory and relish in the truth that He reveals Himself in creation as God of order and love (Romans 1:20). If God is so meticulous that He daily cares for the lilies and sparrows in the field, how much more would He do for you if you just release "you" to His open arms of love?

My spiritual mom, Dr. Bam Crawford has a book set "The Power of the Soul." It is also a deep study of healing. Keep your eyes and ears open to the Lord and pray to see and hear with the eyes and Mind of Christ.

Chapter 3

Living Inside the Rainbow

If we believe we can overcome deep and horrible acts, we can heal from the worst of crimes and live the life that we were always ordained to live. When we rise out of these seemingly insurmountable experiences, we have the potential not only to live anew but also to pull others out of the fire and ashes so that they also may live a new life.

1. Who are you? Briefly state what and who you believe you are...Read and meditate on Proverbs 23:7 "As a man thinketh in his heart so is he."

_____

_____

_____

_____

_____

_____

_____

_____

_____

_____

Identity crisis often leads lots of people into distorted sexual behavior, fornication, pornography, adultery and other sins that affect our life, soul, and health.

2. Did you ever know the love of a mother and father or do you feel you have walked this life all alone without that special connection?

_____

_____

_____

_____

_____

_____

_____

_____

"If my father and mother forsake me, the Lord will take me up," which is far better and healing (Psalm 27:10). It means you're not forsaken; God sees you.

3. Have you ever felt insecure amidst friends? If yes, why?

_____

_____

_____

_____

_____

_____

_____

_____

4. At what age did you become a victim of physical abuse, sex slavery, sexual violence or other rejection, abandonment and trauma? How did it happen? Briefly describe the "hell" you passed through, or are passing through now.

_____

_____

_____

_____

_____

_____

_____

5. Who should take the blame?

Father   Mother   Relative   Society

Me   Friend   Others (specify)_____

6. Why did you choose the answer(s) in 4 above?

_____

_____

_____

_____

_____

_____

_____

_____

We often miss our very own value, beauty, and the wonderment of who we are by judging others and ourselves by outward characteristics.

Is there anyone who you would like to be by your side and comfort you?

_____

_____

_____

_____

_____

_____

8. If there is any, why did you choose him/her?

_____

_____

_____

_____

_____

_____

_____

_____

Life will be what God has already made for you as you lean on Him. I am so sorry for what has happened to you and those you are helping. But God has already made a way of your escape from the clutches of hell to a new life. Only believe and keep fighting. If you are reading this book without going through the educational journey in Living Inside the Rainbow, please get it and use them both on your journey of life's discoveries for you.

Chapter 4

From the Frying Pan into the Fire

I believe with all of my heart that they were bonafide angels.

Is there any voice or has there been anything in your head that keeps telling you negative things? Be very clear. Remember the story from the main book in Chapter 4 if not, read it soon.

_____

_____

_____

_____

_____

_____

_____

_____

2. Mention a few wrong ideologies you were made to believe about yourself under the control of violators, abusers or traffickers.

_____

_____

_____

_____

_____

_____

_____

_____

I thought that I would be loved, somehow. I believed at the time that it was love, and I immediately became addicted to the drugs that were forced on me. Or my father or mother beat me and there was nothing I could do.

3. State any biblical truths that have helped you counter those ideologies or being helpless.

_____

_____

_____

_____

_____

_____

_____

_____

"You shall know the truth and the truth shall set you free" (John 8:32). Meditate on some of the quotes from Chapter 4, in the main book and explore scriptures on truth and freedom. What you hear and see and consciously process in your mind is what you become. That was the secret of human traffickers and abusers: they brainwash their victims so they think its their fault. Use the Word of God to reprogram your mindset.

4. Can you see the love of God for you in that you are a victim to survivor to thriver to champion. Discover what you suffered, with the chance to share a story of victory. Please, write down the scriptures you explored about truth and freedom and meditate on how they affect you and how they apply to your life right now?

_____

_____

_____

_____

_____

_____

_____

5. Celebrate life and state one way you escaped a great moment of danger or premature death.

_____

_____

_____

_____

_____

_____

_____

_____

Even when you were living in sin, God's angels were busy keeping watch over you for a purpose which you must, or have possibly discovered today as a survivor. Read Romans 8:28-30.

6. How will you describe your experience in the hands of violators, abusers or traffickers?

_____

_____

_____

_____

_____

_____

_____

7. Did you see your escape as an act of God or act of man? Try to remember and chronicle the times when you could sense divine intervention. Practice God's presence in your life.

_____

_____

_____

_____

_____

_____

_____

_____

_____

Read Isaiah 42:20. When I did, it was so awesome. The prophet says, "Seeing many things, but thou observest not; opening the ears, but he heareth not."

Don't rush the good things of your life. Think about what God is teaching you and how He desires to change you and cause you to be more and more like Him.

Chapter 5

Reach

I hadn't thought much about any rights I might have had as a human being; and since I had not been saved yet, I surely hadn't thought of what living in the righteousness of God meant.

There is still a place ready for God's people, where they can rest completely. They will rest like God, rested on the seventh day… God rested after He had finished His work. And it is the same for everyone who goes to rest with God. They will rest after they have finished their own work…" (Heb 4:9-10).

1. State what you have come to discover regarding the righteousness of God towards you, in spite of your past.

_____

_____

_____

_____

_____

_____

_____

2. Is there any trend of positive change of lifestyle, behavior and thought life since you are on a journey of discovery about the next best move for your life?

_____

_____

_____

_____

_____

_____

_____

_____

3. Have you ever felt disappointed by God? Why did you feel God let you down even after you poured out your heart and let the past go of why you didn't feel His presence?

_____

_____

_____

_____

_____

_____

_____

_____

All we need do is take the hand, His hand. We may feel like we are walking in the dark, and maybe at times we will be, but not when we are holding the hand of the One who knows exactly who we are and where we need to go.

"...Far be it from God, that He should do wickedness; and from the Almighty, that he should commit iniquity" (Job 34:10).

State how you feel God can use your testimony to change others of all walks of life, even those who are or were in similar types of bondage.

_____

_____

_____

_____

_____

_____

_____

_____

5. What addictions or habits still linger in your life today? Write them down...

_____

_____

_____

_____

_____

_____

_____

...and then hand them over to God. Only God can reach His hand to touch your soul (a combination of your mind, will and emotions).

Cast your burden upon the Lord for He cares for you (1 Peter 5:7). He desires for you to heal.

6. Do you think your prayer life can save those that are still in these bondages? Why or why not?

_____

_____

_____

_____

_____

_____

_____

"...pray one for another, that ye may be healed. The effectual fervent prayer of a righteous man availeth much." (James 5:16)

7. Judging from your experience, what are the ways you think that these abusers, violators and traffickers can be decimated and reduced to the barest minimum?

_____

_____

_____

_____

_____

_____

_____

_____

'If it would destroy [a 12-year-old boy] to be called a girl, what are we then teaching him about girls?' **Tony Porter**

'My people are destroyed for lack of knowledge' (Hos 4:6). Do you know that in spite of the despicable and painful past or present or any mess you find yourself, God still loves you and He wants you to come to rest (Matt 11:28; Titus 2:11)? Do you know that the PURPOSE of God for coming to save the world is because of YOU? Read Matt 9: 9-13.

Do you know that the PURPOSE why Jesus Christ came into the world is to destroy the works of the devil in your life and give you **FREEDOM?** Read 1 John 3:8 & John 10:10. Please write down everything you can think of that you need freedom from? Don't forget to rebuke and release certain spirits such as rejection, anger, bitterness, resentment, selfishness, dualistic behavior, fear, doubt, witchcraft, hate, judgment, unforgiveness and other negativities.

_____

_____

_____

_____

_____

_____

_____

_____

_____

_____

_____

_____

_____

_____

_____

_____

Let not your hearts be troubled, believe in Me (John 14:1-6). Please read and enjoy the rest of your healing journey. Even if you are reading this book to help someone else, we all are on a journey to wholeness.

Chapter 6

The Mind is the Battlefield

But it is also Fought in the Realm of the Supernatural

If then you have been raised with Christ, seek the things that are above, where Christ is seated at the right hand of God. Set your minds on things that are above, not on things that are on earth. For you have died, and your life is hidden with Christ in God. When Christ who is your life appears, then you also will appear with him in glory. (Colossians 3:1-4; ESV)

1. Do you believe God has already changed you and offers you a hope and future?

Read Jeremiah 29:11; Isaiah 62:1-5. Write down the thoughts and impressions that flow easily in your heart and mind.

_____

_____

_____

_____

_____

_____

_____

_____

What God says about you is final—you're loved! You are beautifully and wonderfully made in God's image and likeness. Man's opinion can't define you. So don't allow it to.

2. Take your Bible and read Romans 12:1-3, 2 Corinthians 10:3-6, Proverb 4:23, Colossians 1: 9-14. What did you see?

_____

_____

_____

_____

_____

_____

_____

Your mind is the battle ground; take it over with the thoughts of God and you will find peace and life (Romans 8).

3. Looking at Heb 4:14, how does continuous confession of God's promises conquer your mind from "dead work?"

_____

_____

_____

_____

_____

_____

_____

Knowing that we are the products of what goes on in our mind, how do you renew your mind? Romans 12:2, James 1:21.

_____

_____

_____

_____

_____

_____
_____
_____

4. Do you know that you are clean through the word of God? (John 15: 3).

_____
_____
_____
_____
_____
_____
_____
_____

The gap between where you are and your miracle is renewing your mind continuously with the word of God.

5. What comes to your mind whenever you look at yourself in the mirror? What image of yourself can you see? Be honest…

_____
_____
_____
_____
_____
_____
_____
_____

"A future you cannot picture, you cannot feature"

31

Beautiful things happen to people who believe in beauty
You become a better person by seeing a better you.

6. How often do you hear a voice reminding you of your past?

_____

_____

_____

_____

_____

_____

_____

_____

_____

_____

"He that fears not the future may enjoy the present." - Thomas Fuller

Read 2nd Corinthians 5:17

Meditate and journal of what comes to and flows to
your heart. See you in the next chapter.

Chapter 7

Discovering Sexuality and Goals After Trauma

I believe that children have a certain innate ability to sense and hear God. They are closer to the womb and thus the supernatural, after all. But when that is robbed, when we hurt them and harm one another, life is stifled.

1. Looking back, or looking at society, what can you say about the negative effects associated with the trauma of a child? How has your life been affected by this and what can you do to create and connect your life to a higher purpose?

_____

_____

_____

_____

_____

_____

_____

_____

"But whoso shall offend one of these little ones which believe in me, it were better for him if a millstone were hanged about his neck, and that he were drowned in the depth of the sea." (Matthew 18:6).

2. The formative years of a child falls within the age 1-5. In what ways would you advise parents to raise their kids if you were their advisor, looking at your own experience?

_____

_____

_____
_____
_____
_____
_____
_____
_____

3. What relationship do you treasure most?

_____
_____
_____
_____
_____
_____
_____

Your answer determines who you are now. Oftentimes, the abusers, pedophile trafficker (pimp or madam) will let the children live at home and make them think that the relationship they have is special and secret, as though they still have freedom.

4. If you are a runaway, are you already making contact with relatives who truly care about you? If not, state what stops you from doing just that?

_____
_____
_____
_____
_____
_____
_____

In #3 on the previous page, if your answer is your...
a. abusive boy/girlfriend
b. abuser from family
c. Madam or Pimp/Trafficker
d. a friend whose presence around you lures you into sin,
then you are not free yet. You're still subject to another person's will.

5. As of today, do you have relationships where you are accepted for who you are despite your past? In what ways are you enjoying hope and encouragement from others?

_____
_____
_____
_____
_____
_____
_____
_____

How are, or were, you treated in a local church you once attended when they heard your story?

_____
_____
_____
_____
_____
_____
_____
_____

Sometimes, pastors don't help victims, they become judgmental and pass the blame on to victims seeking counsel. The last thing victims and survivors want to hear is, "What did you do wrong?!" Instead, they should say, "Be restored!"

7. Write the type of future you desire long before abuse.

_____
_____
_____
_____
_____
_____
_____
_____

8. Do you think #7 is still possible?

_____
_____
_____
_____
_____
_____
_____

9. State the reasons for your answer.

_____
_____
_____
_____
_____
_____
_____

"The future belongs to people who believe in the beauty of their dreams."
Read Lamentations 3:26.

"For, I, know the plans which I am planning for you Declareth Yahweh,—Plans of welfare and not of calamity, to give you a future and a hope." (Rotherham)

Chapter 8

The Greatest Gifts Come After Defeat

Salvation is not the gift from a God who does not care about our well-being nor for the poor on the earth who have nothing better, as some writers and speakers have said. It is the reason for life's existence.

In your Bible, read John 4:5-30… Sometimes, because of trauma, we make bad decisions.

Can you relate to that story? Even though it wasn't your fault.

Here, you see the encounter of a Samaritan woman with Jesus Christ at Jacob's well. We could see a broken woman who had distorted sexual behavior, a lady who moved from one abuser to the other, never married the right way.

The conversation Jesus had with her showed she was thirsty for something—there was a vacuum that needed to be filled in her soul, and living a promiscuous life (as she was brainwashed to believe…as those men promised her love) didn't solve her emotional and psychological problem. Could it be that she was being prostituted—considering Judaism which doesn't allow a woman to have many guys in her life? She ought to have been stoned a long time ago according to tradition; yet, God spared her from them that she might meet the Messiah. God came to ambush the traditions of men and bring new life.

Jesus said she would never thirst again if she drank from the Living Water He had to offer.

1. Do you have any sexual/love relationship (out of marriage) with someone, which is difficult to break so you can begin a new life with God? Why do you feel you can't?

_____

_____

_____

_____

_____

_____

_____

_____

_____

Many of us have developed soul ties with ungodly men who raped, violated and hurt others but God can help us break free from the chains. His shed blood on the Cross has the power to set you free if you let Him.

2. If you are, or have ever been in an abusive relationship, why are you looking for love where you will never find it?

_____

_____

_____

_____

_____

_____

_____

3. Can you differentiate between love and physical sex? Explain…

_____

_____

_____

_____
_____
_____
_____
_____

The Samaritan woman had to learn the difference between the water in Jacob's well and the Living Water, and this changed her forever.

4. As a victim seeking deliverance, sit down now and write those negative acts (e.g. smoking, partying, control, addictive actions) you do. Does this satisfy and solve your heart's needs?

_____
_____
_____
_____

5. Now, write good dreams and passion (e.g. becoming an lawyer) you desired (since childhood). Is it obvious to you that your good future is being overtaken by negative patterns?

_____
_____
_____
_____

I felt horrible during and after the acts, acts that were part of my subconscious heart and mind but not part of my hopes or my dreams.

6. If you would drink from the Living Water, you would find peace and rest for your soul right here and now and let the fresh new life in you begin again.

_____
_____

_____

_____

_____

_____

_____

_____

7. Do you know that salvation is the greatest gift you can ever experience in life?

_____

_____

_____

_____

_____

_____

_____

8. How will you describe the peace you enjoy before and after all you've suffered?

_____

_____

_____

_____

_____

_____

_____

9. Do you know that all you have to do is to receive God's love and you don't have to work for it?

_____
_____
_____
_____
_____
_____
_____
_____

10. Did you ever feel loved by and special to God after your experience?

_____
_____
_____
_____
_____
_____
_____

11. If you are to share the gospel with others, how will you use your experience to touch lives?

_____
_____
_____
_____
_____
_____
_____

"If you are unable to use your experience as a catalyst to others' salvation,

then you are not sure of God's love yet."

'But God commendeth his love toward us, in that, while we were yet sinners, Christ died for us.' (Rom 5:8) *Read, study, journal, listen and pray.*

Chapter 9

Being Transformed: Spirit and Science Play A Part

For victims to become survivors and survivors to become thrivers and thrivers to become champions™, we must grow our faith, whatever that means to us right now, we must also learn to be other centered which is imitating God and so much more and then we will begin to experience firsthand our own transformation.

God wants you to be made "whole" in body and soul. Here, I would like to highlight helpful acts you must daily practice so you can live and walk in a supernatural atmosphere of God's presence.

1. Understand and develop faith. Explain how you will change and grow every aspect of your faith to begin to receive God's love, truth and plan for your life?

_____

_____

_____

_____

_____

_____

_____

_____

2. Deal with negative emotions trying to flow from your past to your now. Remember you are not your emotions.

_____

_____

_____

_____

_____

_____

_____

_____

Many victims of sex slavery, abuse, and violence complain they have thoughts of suicide, anxiety, lack of feelings, self-hatred, mental confusion, low self-esteem, drug addiction, and trust issues. Some abused children are so angry that they get involved in a number of crimes, including serious gang warfare, aiding and abetting criminals, burglary, extreme violence, murder, and rape. Anger and bitterness take on different outlets if we allow it and so we need to release it.

3. Spend time in communion with God. Find a quiet place where you have solitude and wait upon the Lord—let heaven's dew distill upon your head and soothe your soul. Read Isaiah 40:28-31.

_____

_____

_____

_____

_____

_____

_____

_____

4. You might change your type of music. You might become use to lustful, sensual and sexually provoking hard lyrics and songs. Find worship songs that lift the soul to God. Calming, soaking songs, apart from being spiritually edifying, have therapeutic effects on the mind.

_____
_____
_____
_____
_____
_____
_____
_____

5. Mediate on Scriptures day and night. *"They are spirit and they are life"* (John 6:63). Read Joshua 1:8.

_____
_____
_____
_____
_____
_____
_____

6. Eat well!

_____
_____
_____
_____
_____
_____

7. Exercise and rest as appropriate.

_____
_____

_____

_____

_____

_____

_____

_____

Now that you love God and yourself, "glorify God in your spirit and in your body, which are God's" (1 Corinthians 6:20).

Chapter 10

Letting Go

Having got out of your past chains, look inward and see how God has blessed you with gifts and abilities you couldn't explore while in bondage.

1. Mention the spiritual gifts you have discovered in your life as God's special endowment.

_____

_____

_____

_____

_____

_____

_____

_____

Read Romans 12:3-8, 1 Corinthians 12:4-31, 1 Peter 4:10-11.

2. In a few words, who is Jesus to you?

_____

_____

_____

_____

_____

_____

_____

_____

The hidden riches of life for me were knowing Jesus, and through Him, and the Holy Spirit, discovering who I was; my personality, my opinions, destiny, witness, understanding, knowledge, intelligence, abilities, spiritual gifts, and my IDENTITY.

3. Is there anything God wants you to give up so that you can discover your God identity and you still have doubts in your mind?

_____

_____

_____

_____

_____

_____

_____

_____

_____

"Not as I will but as you will of God."

4. Write down positive, godly things God has said about you to counter what you or others say or think about you.

_____

_____

_____

_____

_____

_____

_____

5. What do you understand by your eye (your conscience) being single? Luke 11:34

_____

_____

_____
_____
_____
_____
_____
_____

6. State what you need to do continuously to mortify your body?'

_____
_____
_____
_____
_____
_____
_____

7. What other talents/gifts do you have that can be of help if you will draw near to God?

_____
_____
_____
_____
_____
_____
_____

8. Write down three ways by which you can let go of the past.

_____
_____
_____

_____

_____

_____

_____

_____

9. Growth is gradual while overcoming the past comes slowly by conscious and constant effort towards change, state three practical ways by which these can be achieved.

_____

_____

_____

_____

_____

_____

_____

_____

_____

Chapter 11

Hearing the Holy Spirit

I cannot live without His presence.

1. Have you received the Holy Spirit since you believed? If yes, recount your experience.

_____

_____

_____

_____

_____

_____

_____

_____

If no, do this (I suggest):
i. Get a believer to pray with you.
ii. Ask Father God in faith and wait upon Him.

The Holy Spirit is coming upon you now! The COMFORTER is highly essential to every survivor of sexual violence and any abuse or violence. *What the Holy Spirit does, for lack of the fullness of the root word, is to comfort.*

2. From what you have learned so far in Living Inside The Rainbow's main book, mention 5-7 ways the Holy Spirit can be of help to *you*. Hint: Include Bible references.

_____

_____

_____

_____

_____

_____

_____

_____

3. Having direction for your life is a key to peace. How have you been able to discern God's voice? Mention specific experiences/incidents wherein the Holy Spirit gave you guidance.

_____

_____

_____

_____

_____

_____

_____

_____

There are many ways in which God speaks to us, and we need to spend time with Him to be able to hear His Spirit.

4. Mention ways by which the Holy Spirit relates with you?

_____

_____

_____

_____

_____

_____

_____

5. Have you received the baptism of the Holy Spirit?

_____

_____

_____

_____

_____

_____

_____

6. Do you know that the gift of the Holy Spirit is for all that believe? Act 2:38-39

_____

_____

_____

_____

_____

_____

_____

7. Identify the ways the gifts of the spirit aided your recovery and restoration or can if you allow?

_____

_____

_____

_____

_____

_____

_____

Chapter 12

The Need for Fathers

Without a Father, you cannot go farther

1. What values/beliefs do you hold on family life in general?

_____

_____

_____

_____

_____

_____

_____

_____

2. For Women:

a. What are your expectations from a Man as husband and father in the home?

_____

_____

_____

_____

_____

_____

b. Who are you? State what it means to be a Woman or Mother. Hint: tell of what you know about womanhood as God says it.

_____
_____
_____
_____
_____
_____
_____

3. For Men:

a. What are the roles of a Woman in a family and in life?

_____
_____
_____
_____
_____
_____
_____

b. Do you know what it means to be a Man or Father (figure) in a home or in life setting? Explain your views.

_____
_____
_____
_____
_____
_____

One of the fundamental reason for having troubled homes is lack of understanding of what a marriage relationship entails—in terms of husband-wife and parent-child responsibilities. Check your answers against Scriptures. You may want to visit a relationship advisor for help. What we don't know is killing family life today. See The Importance of Fathers: Statistical compilation by the South Carolina Fathers Initiative by Keith Pounds; pages 216-218.

4. State how your home environment contributed to your experience of of pain and trauma?

_____

_____

_____

_____

_____

_____

_____

_____

5. As a parent, if there is anything you would like to make right today, what would it be?

_____

_____

_____

_____

_____

_____

_____

_____

6. As a child who had little or no experience of love from parents, would you rather learn from their mistakes (including yours) so you can be a good role model for your own kids? What would you do differently?

_____

_____

_____

_____

_____

_____

_____

_____

_____

7. State the expectation of God for fathers in the home, workplace and the community?

_____

_____

_____

_____

_____

_____

_____

_____

8. How will you explain the' father-figure' in family and society?

_____

_____

_____

_____

_____

_____

_____

_____

Chapter 13

Our Language is Our Life

As well as healing and changing our lives after abuse and challenges, we must also change our very language about these related issues, if we are truly to thrive.

If we must fight against violence, rape, sex slavery, human trafficking in today's society, we must not call good evil and evil good. More so, just as words were used to brainwash victims, so also words are important to your emotional and mental healing.

Confession, based on God's word, is very powerful and effectual in the process of recovery.

Point of Action: Each day, learn to confess Scripture and affirm God's word about you.

1. In the space below, write out a confession of good, positive, and edifying things (e.g. Psalm 139:14) you desire in respect of Scripture and what you've learned so far in Living Inside the Rainbow.

_____

_____

_____

_____

_____

_____

_____

2. What values and beliefs do you hold on human sexuality regarding the following that are very common today? This is not about judging but

oftentimes, myself included, all of the abuse as a young girl caused me to question my sexuality and many said I was born a certain way but I knew I wasn't, I was only afraid of men because of what happened.

a. How do you feel about Homosexuality

_____
_____
_____
_____
_____
_____
_____
_____

b. Homesexuality/Lesbianism

_____
_____
_____
_____
_____
_____
_____
_____

c. Transgender

_____
_____
_____
_____
_____

d. Bisexuality

_____
_____
_____
_____
_____
_____
_____
_____

What about certain crimes such as:

e. Rape

_____
_____
_____
_____
_____
_____
_____
_____

f. Incest

_____
_____
_____
_____
_____
_____
_____
_____

g. Pedophilia

_____
_____
_____
_____
_____
_____
_____

h. Prostitution

_____
_____
_____
_____
_____
_____
_____

i. Porn: America is the number one producer of child porn

_____
_____
_____
_____
_____
_____
_____

Confused views on human sexuality because of trauma we face and sex-related behaviors make young people more susceptible to sex slavery and abuse, domestic violence and trauma.

How can societies diverse perspective on these issues reflect the true picture of a loving and healthy lifestyle for you? (Find your own voice)

_____
_____
_____
_____
_____
_____
_____
_____
_____

4. Suggest the right words/names to call the 'violated persons' that can boost their self-esteem without making assumptions.

_____
_____
_____
_____
_____
_____
_____
_____

5. What do you think should be a parent's attitude towards the sexualities mentioned in (2)?

_____
_____
_____
_____

_____
_____
_____
_____

6. How will you react if you are called a troubled person, sex slave or victim by a friend?

_____
_____
_____
_____
_____
_____
_____
_____

7. Suggest ways to eliminate completely, the wrong tag placed on people who have been hurt just like you and me.

_____
_____
_____
_____
_____
_____
_____

Chapter 14

Reconciliation

Only love and God-breathed wisdom, rooted in the kindness and prudence of divine experience, education and being in accord with mutual listening and awareness, can heal disorders within our society.

"In order to escape accountability for his crimes, the perpetrator does everything in his power to promote forgetting. If secrecy fails, the perpetrator attacks the credibility of his victim. If he cannot silence her absolutely, he tries to make sure no one listens."

— Judith Lewis Herman

God has asked us to listen and to seek justice by fighting for orphans, widows, the homeless, the fatherless and often, it is us.

1. Mention some dividing lines that do not foster unity toward fighting and curbing abuse and sexual violent crimes and other violence in your state, country or neighborhood.

_____

_____

_____

_____

_____

_____

_____

_____

2. How does political leadership and law enforcement agencies in your state, city or country handle cases related to sexual perversion and other violence? Is there any hope for victims?

_____

_____

_____

_____

_____

_____

_____

_____

3. Is there any support group or program in your area that provides help to victims , perpetrators and those suffering?

_____

_____

_____

_____

_____

_____

_____

_____

With all of the rescues and stings in the USA, children and boys, girls and women need a place to go and heal—a place run by people who truly understand what they've been through.

4. Can you affirm that you're now a healthy survivor or are assisting one?

_____

_____

_____

_____

_____

_____

_____

_____

If yes, get trained and become fit to assist former victims of human trafficking and sexual violence who are still hurting. See Jude 1:23, 2 Corinthians 1:3-6.

5. Do you think you can be a voice for former victims by starting a group that will champion the cause or maybe volunteer?

_____
_____
_____
_____
_____
_____
_____
_____

Who will rise up for me against the evildoers? or who will stand up for me against the workers of iniquity? (Psalm 94:16)

If so, why don't you join a program today, something like brookbello.com or moretoolife.org? Also learn how you can help men and young men learn about sexual violence prevention and also provide education to violators. Learn more about my RJEDE® Program Restorative Justice End Demand Education. Please give me a call at 941-227-1012.

Conclusion

Who knew that my life would be a hidden treasure, my Lord was waiting to show me! In Him, my life would be my treasure found on the other side of the rainbow. The rainbow in the sky throughout my life would be a glimpse into His presence.

You were created for greatness; so believe it, accept it, and pursue it. Your past is past, and the true light of who you really are now shines forth. God has made a new vessel out of you—and the vessel is full of His treasure—to showcase His glory on earth. Read Jeremiah 18:1-6; 2 Corinthians 4:5-7.

Author's Bio:

Author, actress and motivational speaker and preacher, Abolitionist and Rev, Dr. Brook Bello is passionate. As an actor artist and film-maker she has been in dozens of TV shows and films. Brook, is also the founder of YOUTHIASM® A ministry that deals with freedom, on all levels and mental & soul health and being youthfully enthusiastic about the things of God. On the Oprah Winfrey Network, Dr. Bello was chosen 1 of 10 national heroes in a series by Dolphin Digital Media and United Way Worldwide called, The Hero Effect." She and her agency, More Too Life's, expertise is evident in many ways. More Too Life is an award winning anti-sexual violence, human trafficking and youth crime prevention organization that was named by United Way World Wide as one of the best in the nation. Bello, the founder received the highest award from the President of the United States and the White House in December 2016 for the innovative and profound work in victim services and prevention of victims and youth and adult men related to human trafficking and sexual violence. She also received advocate of the year in the state of Florida presented in 2017 by A.G. Pam Bondi and Gov. Rick Scott, Bello received 2 honoree doctorates and is complete with an earned third doctorate in Pastoral Clinical Counseling from Covenant Theological Seminary. Bello is a licensed chaplain with CICA International University and Seminary accredited by the only NGO accredited by the United Nations to do so, she has also received accreditation and licensing in temperance couseling from NCCA (National Christian Counseling Association) Bello, teaches and preaches around the world a message of love, hope, freedom and the urgency of socially conscience innovation and legislation. Speaking engagements include: The White House, The Carter Center, Rotary International, United Way Worldwide, Wheelock College, Georgetown University, Miles College, Dominguez Hills University, UCLA, First Baptist Church Glenarden Underground Railroad Freedom Center, Womens Equality Day, Festival De Cannes and so many many others.

Order other Books by Dr. Brook Parker Bello